Kuo Huey Jen

Wok Specialities

Cookery Editor Sonia Allison

Series Editor Wendy Hobson

foulsham

Preface

Wok cookery has become almost a byword for Far Eastern cuisine. In a short space of time, its use has spread almost worldwide and it is now at home in kitchens from Peking to London to New York.

Woks can be used for all kinds of different cooking methods: stir-frying, deep-frying, frying pastry parcels, basting, braising, steaming and boiling. The variety of Chinese cooking is astonishing and food prepared in the wok is delicious. So go ahead and try some of these wonderful recipes and you will soon be impressed with how easy, versatile and tasty wok cookery can be.

Contents

An Introduction to Far Eastern Cuisine

The wok and Chinese cooking go hand in hand and no other kitchen utensil is as widely used for Far Eastern cuisine. If you are not familiar with using a wok, you can soon learn how simple it is to get good results.

Choosing and Using a Wok

Resembling an upturned coolie hat or hollow hemisphere and made from metal, the wok is widely available from department stores and speciality shops at reasonable cost and in a range of sizes to suit differing family needs. Although not strictly authentic by Oriental standards, there are even non-stick woks, and electric woks which are thermostatically-controlled, trouble-free to use and easy to clean.

The wok is suitable for practically all traditional Chinese cooking methods and is the ideal choice for stir-frying. Additionally it can also be used for deep and shallow frying, braising, stewing, steaming and boiling.

When you are choosing a wok, make sure that it is sturdy and made from strong metal such as cast iron or stainless steel. Cast iron is said to be preferable because food sticks less to it, but either way the pan should be heavy enough not to topple or tip over while in use. Some woks have a metal handle on either side, others a wooden handle on one side.

A wok gives more satisfactory results if placed over a gas flame rather than an electric ring. Those with electric hobs are advised to use a separate, plug-in electric wok.

To steady the wok while in use, a sensible precaution is to invest in a wok ring on which the wok can sit. This looks like a curved flan ring, but is deeper with perforations all the way round. The ring should NOT be used when stir frying as the base of the wok needs to be in direct contact with the heat source for fast cooking.

Although woks are available in assorted sizes, the very large ones are unsuitable for home use as the distribution of heat from base to sides will be uneven and inade-quate. Choose one measuring about 30 to 38 cm/12 to 15 in in diameter.

A lid to go with the wok is useful for wet methods of cooking: steaming, stewing, braising and simmering. Choose a well-fitting, deep lid so that a chicken or duck can be accommodated underneath without gaps round the sides. The lid is usually made from a lighter metal than the wok itself.

Before using, 'season' the wok by washing, oiling and heating. Firstly wash out with hot detergent water. Pour out, rinse with hot water and wipe inside of wok dry. Using a brush, coat inside with groundnut or sesame oil. Heat until hot. Take off heat and, when cool enough to handle, wipe clean with kitchen paper. Repeat the oiling and heating three or four more times or until paper remains unblackened. Finally wipe with a little oil (unless in daily use when this will be unnecessary) and hang up in a warm spot in the kitchen. Before using, rinse out with very hot water and dry thoroughly. Under no circumstances attempt to 'season' a non-stick wok or the surface will be damaged.

For protection, use oven gloves when working with a wok as the handles can

6

become extremely hot.

Before cooking in the wok, make sure it has been thoroughly heated and the oil for frying is at kitchen temperature.

About the Recipes

1 Do not mix metric, Imperial or American measures.

2 Spoon measurements are level.

3 Eggs are size 3.

4 Preparation times include both preparation and cooking times and are approximate.

5 Temperatures given are for conventional ovens. Check with manufacturers' handbook for other types of oven.

6 You can use Szechuan pepper for an authentic taste, but black pepper is an acceptable substitute.

7 Ingredients are available in major supermarkets or Oriental shops.

8 Seasoning is very much a matter of taste, so do taste.

Utensils

Flat Ladle or Spatula

Looking a bit like a shovel, this is a cross between a wide palette knife and shallow ladle. It is made from metal, usually stainless steel, and is flattish with slightly raised edges on either side. The front is curved slightly outwards and it has a long handle. The ladle is used mainly for turning foods over in the wok and lifting cooked items out of the pan.

Wire Ladle or Strainer

Attached to a wooden handle, this is a cup-shaped utensil made from mesh. It comes in various sizes and is frequently used in conjunction with the wok. See photographs pages 8 and 9.

Steamers

Made from wood and bamboo, these can be found in an assortment of sizes but all are round and geared to fit on top of the wok or inside it. They are easy to stack, one on top of the other, enabling several different foods to be kept separate while they are cooked at the same time. All steamers should be covered, either with bamboo lids or lid of the wok, while the foods are being cooked.

Cooking Methods

Frying
Small pieces of food can easily be shallow fried in the wok. Do not fill the wok too full while frying.

Braising
Cut-up pieces of food (not too large) can be simmered in a small amount of liquid. The technique is to add the liquid gradually and continue to cook until it has completely evaporated. The process should be repeated until all the liquid or marinade recommended in the recipe has been used up.

Stir-Frying
Bite-sized pieces of meat can be fried quickly in a little hot oil over a high heat. The technique is to stir the food continuously, either with a ladle or with chopsticks as shown. It is important to add the foods in the correct order so that all the ingredients complete cooking at the same time. For instance, meat should be added first, fresh mushrooms last.

Deep-Frying
Seasoned pieces of uncoated food are best deep fried in a wire ladle or strainer so that they can be removed and drained quickly.

Deep-Frying ②
Pastry-wrapped food, also in fairly small pieces, is delicious deep-fried in oil. An example here would be spring rolls. This same method of frying is used for ingredients coated with breadcrumbs, egg batter, flour or cornflour.

Frying and Basting
Fast-cooking foods, held in a wire strainer or ladle, can be continually basted with oil while frying.

Stewing in Liquid
Popular in the south of China, this picture shows meat and vegetables being cooked in stock or water until both are tender. The meat should be cooked before the vegetables and the wok kept covered.

Simmering
Small strips and pieces of fine quality and tender foods should again be held in a wire ladle or strainer, and basted with hot liquid until cooked through.

Steaming
Blanched foods are cooked in a small bamboo steamer placed inside the wok with the liquid. For more detail, see steamers under Utensils on page 6.

Combination Boiling and Frying
Small pieces of already-cooked food can be tenderised by steaming in a basket.

Combination Frying and Steaming
Pieces of crisply-fried foods can be tenderised by steaming in a basket.

Marinating
In many Chinese recipes, pieces of food are left to soak (or marinate) in a marinade or savoury liquid prior to cooking. The marinade is sometimes used to baste the food while it is being cooked or treated as a sauce base.

9

Chinese Cooking Ingredients

Most of the following ingredients are available from major supermarkets or Oriental food shops.

Oyster Sauce ⑦
This thick, spicy sauce is made from oysters and is especially popular for use in fish cookery. Like crab sauce, it is available in small tins or in bottles. Both sauces can be kept in the refrigerator for many months.

Bean Sauce ⑤
Bean sauce is very thick and is sold either as yellow or red bean sauce.

Chilli Oil ⑧
In China, this oil is generally home-made. Dried or fresh chilli peppers are roasted in a little oil for 5 to 10 minutes, left until cold then strained with the oil through muslin or filter paper before being transferred to a stoppered bottle or jar. Left in the cool, the oil will retain its heat and flavour for about a month.

Chinese Mushrooms ⑥
Oriental shops now offer a large selection of dried mushrooms. Before use they must be soaked until soft, then cut up according to the instructions in the recipe. Care should be taken with quantities, as only about 15 g/¹/₂ oz are sufficient when used in a recipe for, say, 4 people.

The best known mushrooms are probably the cloud's ear, as well as grass mushrooms, morels, straw mushrooms or Tongu mushrooms, also known as Chinese champignons.

Spices ⑫
Although five-spice powder is easily obtainable, some recipes call for the spice mixture of your choice instead. The main ingredients are star anise, cloves, ginger, cardamom, coriander, pimento, pepper and cinnamon. If preferred, whole spices can be crushed with a pestle and mortar and used fresh.

Clear Noodles ①
Clear, glass or cellophane

noodles make an excellent accompaniment to Chinese food, but check cooking directions as sometimes the noodles need soaking before boiling. They can also be fried in very hot oil. This type of noodle is usually made from mung bean flour.

Hoisin Sauce ③

Hoisin sauce is made from pumpkin, soy beans, garlic and spices. It is thick and hot, but also has a slightly sweet taste.

Oil ⑩ and ⑪ .

In general, groundnut oil (peanut oil) is used in Oriental cooking as it can be heated to a high temperature without deterioration. It should be carefully strained after use and reserved for further frying – about two or three more times at the most. Sesame oil, also very popular, tends to be on the expensive side and is therefore kept for flavouring. For instance, 10 ml/2 tsp added to noodles or a stir-fry dish gives it a warm, smoky and aromatic taste.

Plum Sauce ②

Plum sauce is also called duck sauce as it is the usual accompaniment for Peking Duck. You can buy tins or bottles of this fruity sauce from most supermarkets.

Soy Sauce ⑨

Soy sauce is a strong, dark cooking sauce made from soy beans and flavourings. Caramel gives it its rich dark colour and the sauce is not only used in recipes but also as an accompaniment to made-up Chinese dishes. Light soy sauce is paler and more aromatic.

Szechuan Pepper ④

Szechuan pepper is produced from a dark red berry with a distinctive fragrance – rather like a mixture of lavender and ginger. For maximum aroma, bags of imported Chinese peppercorns should be sprinkled, a few at a time, across the base of a non-stick frying pan and dry-fried for 4 minutes. After cooking, they can be transferred to a pepper mill and then ground into dishes as recommended in the recipes.

Aromatic Fried Dishes

This chapter gives you a delicious selection of dishes which can be stir-fried to perfection in the wok.

Fiery Strips of Pork Fillet, page 14

Fiery Strips of Pork Fillet

Serves 4
Preparation time: 30 mins
plus marinating
1900 kcal/7980 kJ

---

500 g/1 1/4 lb pork fillet, cut into strips

30 ml/2 tbsp soy sauce

30 ml/2 tbsp Hoisin sauce

5 ml/1 tsp five-spice powder

15 ml/1 tbsp black pepper, coarsely ground

15 ml/1 tbsp brown sugar

15 ml/1 tbsp sesame oil

30 ml/2 tbsp groundnut oil

1 bunch spring onions, chopped

1 red pepper, cut into strips

1 green pepper, cut into strips

1 x 200 g/7 oz small tin beansprouts, drained

2 slices fresh or tinned pineapple, diced

45 ml/3 tbsp tomato ketchup

150 ml/1/4 pt/2/3 cup chicken stock

salt and Szechuan pepper

---

1 Marinate the meat with the sauces, spices and sugar for 30 minutes.
2 Sizzle the oils in a wok, add the meat and quickly stir-fry until light golden brown. Remove the meat from the wok.
3 Add the vegetables and fry. Add the pineapple, tomato ketchup and stock. Bring to the boil.
4 Return the meat to the wok, stir and season.

Photograph page 12

Pork Strips with Vegetables

Serves 4
Preparation time: 30 mins
1500 kcal/6300 kJ

---

2 cloves garlic

salt

2.5 ml/1/2 tsp Szechuan pepper

30 ml/2 tbsp groundnut oil

450 g/1 lb lean pork loin, cut into strips

30 ml/2 tbsp soy sauce

225 g/8 oz broccoli florets

200 g/7 oz cauliflower florets

1 red pepper, diced

1 onion, chopped

2 oranges, peeled and diced

1 piece stem ginger in syrup, chopped

25 ml/1 1/2 tbsp cornflour smoothly mixed with 300 ml/ 1/2 pt/1 1/4 cups cold water

30 ml/2 tbsp vinegar

15 ml/1 tbsp honey

a pinch of powdered ginger

2.5 ml/1/2 tsp cumin

Szechuan pepper

---

1 Crush the garlic with the salt and rub well into the meat with the pepper.
2 Heat the oil in a wok and stir-fry the meat. Remove the meat from the wok and keep it warm.
3 Add the soy sauce to the remaining oil and use it to fry the vegetables until they are just tender but still crisp. Add the oranges, stem ginger and cornflour mixture and stir in. Then add the vinegar, honey, ginger and cumin.

Season to taste with salt and pepper if necessary.
4 Return the meat to the wok and reheat, stirring continuously and keeping the heat fairly brisk.

Photograph opposite (top)

Marinated Pork

Serves 4
Preparation time: 50 mins
2340 kcal/9830 kJ

---

500 g/1 1/4 lb stewing pork, diced

2 cloves garlic, crushed

salt

60 ml/4 tbsp tomato ketchup

30 ml/2 tbsp soy sauce

30 ml/2 tbsp plum sauce

5 ml/1 tsp curry powder

5 ml/1 tsp paprika

2.5 ml/1/2 tsp Szechuan pepper

45 ml/3 tbsp groundnut oil

1 bunch spring onions, cut into strips

4 medium carrots, cut into narrow strips

---

1 Marinate the meat with the garlic, salt, tomato ketchup, sauces and spices for 20 minutes.
2 Heat the oil in a wok and fry the meat well. Remove the meat from the wok.
3 Add the vegetables to the remaining oil and fry until cooked. Add the meat, reheat briefly, season to taste and serve.

Photograph opposite (bottom)

15

Diced Chicken in Peanut Butter

Serves 4
Preparation time: 30 mins
1630 kcal/6850 kJ

4 chicken breast fillets, diced

salt and Szechuan pepper

5 ml/**1 tsp** five-spice powder

45 ml/**3 tbsp** groundnut oil

1 onion, diced

2 carrots, diced

1 stalk celery, diced

300 ml/¹/₂ **pt**/1 ¹/₄ cups chicken stock, hot

10 ml/**2 tsp** tomato purée

100 g/**4 oz** peanut butter

15 ml/**1 tbsp** soy sauce

10 ml/**2 tsp** cornflour

a few drops of vinegar

a pinch of brown sugar

15 ml/**1 tbsp** finely chopped chives

1 Season the chicken breast with salt, Szechuan pepper and five-spice powder.
2 Heat the oil in a wok and stir-fry the chicken until tender. Remove the chicken from the wok and keep it warm.
3 Add the vegetables to the oil and fry until cooked. Mix the chicken stock with the tomato purée, peanut butter, soy sauce and cornflour. Add this to the vegetables and bring to the boil.
3 Return the chicken to the wok and reheat. Season with vinegar and sugar and sprinkle with chives.

Photograph (top)

Sweet-Sour Duck

Serves 4
Preparation time: 2 hours
plus chilling
3900 kcal/16380 kJ

1 oven-ready duck	
Stock:	
*1.2 l/2 **pts**/5 cups chicken stock*	
2 onions, whole	
2 carrots, whole	
2 cloves garlic, sliced	
*15 ml/1 **tbsp** pickling spice*	
*10 ml/2 **tsp** salt*	
*10 ml/2 **tsp** groundnut oil*	
1 bunch spring onions, chopped	
1 fresh mango, cubed	
12 lychees, halved	
*15 ml/1 **tbsp** cornflour*	
*15 ml/1 **tbsp** vinegar*	
*10 ml/2 **tsp** tomato purée*	
*15 ml/1 **tbsp** soy sauce*	
*5 ml/1 **tsp** five-spice powder*	
*300 ml/^{1}/$_2$ **pt**/1 ^{1}/$_4$ cups chicken stock, hot*	

1 Arrange the duck in a steam basket over a wok containing the stock ingredients. Cover and steam for 2^1/$_2$ hours, topping up with boiling stock.
2 Cool the duck, cover and chill for 6 hours. Remove the meat from the bones and cut into cubes.
3 Sizzle the oil in a clean wok. Add the duck and spring onions and stir-fry until crisp. Stir in the remaining ingredients and bring to the boil. Simmer for 2 minutes.

Photograph (bottom right)

Chinese Cabbage with Mushrooms

Serves 4
Preparation time: 25-30 mins
1960 kcal/8230 kJ

45 ml/*3 tbsp* groundnut oil
1 medium Chinese cabbage, diced
1 red pepper, diced
1 green pepper, diced
6 Chinese mushrooms, soaked and cut into strips
225 g/*8 oz* air-dried garlic sausage, diced small
120 ml/*4 fl oz*/¹/₂ cup chicken stock
45 ml/*3 tbsp* vinegar
20 ml/*4 tsp* soy sauce
20 ml/*4 tsp* honey
5 ml/*1 tsp* cornflour
salt
Szechuan pepper
30 ml/*2 tbsp* finely chopped chives

1 Heat the oil in a wok, add vegetables and stir-fry for about 5 minutes.
2 Add the garlic sausage and fry briefly. Mix the chicken stock with the vinegar, soy sauce, honey and cornflour. Stir until smooth. Add to the vegetables and bring to the boil.
3 Season to taste with salt and a few grindings of pepper, then serve sprinkled with chives.

Photograph opposite (top right)

Fried Spring Vegetables

Serves 4
Preparation time: 25 mins
960 kcal/4030 kJ

1 bunch spring onions, chopped
1 red pepper, cut into strips
1 green pepper, cut into strips
100 g/*4 oz* beansprouts
225 g/*8 oz* mange-tout, each chopped into 4 pieces
45 ml/*3 tbsp* groundnut oil
2 cloves garlic
salt
30 ml/*2 tbsp* soy sauce
30 ml/*2 tbsp* Hoisin sauce
5 ml/*1 tsp* tomato purée
5 ml/*1 tsp* cornflour
120 ml/*4 fl oz*/¹/₂ cup chicken stock
Szechuan pepper
a few drops of lemon juice
60 ml/*4 tbsp* chopped chives

1 Wash the vegetables under running water and pat dry.
2 Heat the oil in a wok. Crush the garlic with the salt, then add to the oil with the sauces and heat through.
3 Add the vegetables to the wok and cook, stirring continuously, until they are just tender but still crisp.
4 Stir the tomato purée and cornflour into the chicken stock, add to the vegetables and bring to the boil. Season to taste with a few grindings of pepper and the lemon juice and serve sprinkled with chives.

Photograph opposite (top left)

Fried Rice with Ground Beef

Serves 4
Preparation time: 20-25 mins
2760 kcal/11590 kJ

1 clove garlic
salt
30 ml/*2 tbsp* groundnut oil
30 ml/*2 tbsp* soy sauce
30 ml/*2 tbsp* Hoisin sauce
Szechuan pepper, coarsely ground
450 g/*1 lb* lean ground beef
1 onion, diced
2 carrots, diced
1 leek, diced
450 g/*1 lb* boiled rice (about 150 g/*5 oz* when uncooked)

1 Crush the garlic with the salt and heat with the oil in a wok for 1 or 2 minutes. Add the sauces and 2 or 3 grindings of pepper.
2 Add the beef and fry well, stirring continuously until brown and crumbly. Add the vegetables and fry until cooked.
3 Adjust the seasoning to taste and add the boiled rice to the meat. Fry, stirring continuously, for 3 minutes.

Photograph opposite (bottom)

19

Fried Noodles

Serves 4
Preparation time: 15 mins
1230 kcal/5170 kJ

20 ml/*4 tsp* sesame oil	
1 bunch spring onions, cut into strips	
1 red pepper, cut into strips	
6 Chinese mushrooms, soaked and cut into strips	
juice of 1 lemon	
225 g/*8 oz* shrimps or prawns, thawed if frozen	
20 ml/*4 tsp* soy sauce	
20 ml/*4 tsp* oyster sauce	
400 g/*14 oz* cooked Chinese noodles (about 120 g/*4¹/₂ oz* when uncooked)	
salt and Szechuan pepper	
30 ml/*2 tbsp* chopped chives	

1 Heat the oil in a wok, add the vegetables and stir-fry for 3 to 4 minutes.
2 Squeeze the lemon juice over the shrimps or prawns and add to the vegetables with the soy and oyster sauces.
3 Add the well-drained noodles and fry, stirring continuously until heated through. Season to taste with salt and 2 or 3 gridings of pepper and finally sprinkle with chives.

Photograph (left)

Far Eastern Style Prawns

Serves 4
Preparation time: 20 mins
plus marinating
1400 kcal/5880 kJ

16-20 king prawn tails or scampi, peeled
juice of 1 lemon
120 ml/4 fl oz/¹/₂ cup dry white wine
*30 ml/2 **tbsp** soy sauce*
*30 ml/2 **tbsp** honey*
*15 ml/1 **tbsp** grated lemon rind*
salt, Szechuan pepper
*45 ml/3 **tbsp** groundnut oil*
1 clove garlic, chopped
1 bunch spring onions, cut into strips
2 carrots, cut into strips
*5 ml/1 **tsp** five-spice powder*
*5 ml/1 **tsp** cornflour*

1 Mix the prawn tails or scampi with the lemon juice, wine, soy sauce, honey and lemon rind. Season with salt and pepper and marinate for 1 hour in a covered dish.
2 Heat the oil in a wok with the garlic. Add the vegetables and stir-fry until just tender but still crisp. Mix in the drained prawns and cook for 2 minutes.
3 Strain the marinade and mix it smoothly with the five-spice powder and cornflour. Add to the wok, stir in well and bring just up to the boil. Adjust the seasoning to taste.

Photograph (right)

Lamb with Vegetables

Serves 4
Preparation time: 30 mins plus marinating
1550 kcal/6510 kJ

---

500 g/1 1/4 lb lamb fillet, cut into strips

15 ml/1 tbsp sesame oil

30 ml/2 tbsp honey

30 ml/2 tbsp mild vinegar

30 ml/2 tbsp soy sauce

5 ml/1 tsp five-spice powder

15 ml/1 tbsp groundnut oil

1/2 bunch spring onions, chopped

225 g/8 oz fresh bean sprouts

1 red pepper, cut into strips

4 slices fresh pineapple, diced

30 ml/2 tbsp tomato purée

salt and Szechuan pepper

---

1 Marinate the lamb with the sesame oil, honey, vinegar, soy sauce and five-spice powder for at least 2 hours. Transfer the lamb to a plate.
2 Heat the groundnut oil in a wok and stir-fry the lamb for 7 to 9 minutes or until cooked. Remove the lamb from the wok.
3 Add the vegetables and pineapple to the wok and fry, stirring until tender but crisp.
4 Stir in the meat and tomato purée, season and bring just up to the boil before serving.

Photograph opposite (bottom)

Duck with Exotic Fruits

Serves 4
Preparation time: 30 mins plus marinating
1520 kcal/6380 kJ

---

4 duck breast fillets, cut into strips

2.5 ml/1/2 tsp five-spice powder

30 ml/2 tbsp soy sauce

15 ml/1 tbsp sesame oil

15 ml/1 tbsp groundnut oil

2 stalks celery, diced

2 slices tinned pineapple, diced

100 g/4 oz melon, diced

100 g/4 oz lychees, halved

120 ml/4 fl oz/1/2 cup chicken stock

30 ml/2 tbsp tomato purée

30 ml/2 tbsp Hoisin sauce

10 ml/2 tsp vinegar

a pinch of brown sugar

salt and Szechuan pepper

---

1 Marinate the duck with the five-spice powder, soy sauce and sesame oil for at least 2 hours.
2 Heat the groundnut oil in a wok, add the duck and stir-fry for 8 to 10 minutes. Remove the duck from the wok.
3 Add the celery and fruits to the wok and fry, stirring for 4 minutes.
4 Return the duck to the wok with the remaining ingredients and bring to the boil. Simmer for 2 minutes, stirring.

Photograph opposite (centre)

Venison with Cloud's Ear Mushrooms

Serves 4
Preparation time: 25 mins plus marinating
1250 kcal/5250 kJ

---

500 g/1 1/4 lb fillet of venison, cut into strips

15 ml/1 tbsp juniper berries, coarsely ground

15 ml/1 tbsp sesame oil

30 ml/2 tbsp soy sauce

30 ml/2 tbsp Hoisin sauce

5 ml/1 tsp five-spice powder

30 ml/2 tbsp groundnut oil

1 bunch spring onions, chopped

8 cloud's ear mushrooms, soaked and cut into strips

30 ml/2 tbsp honey

30 ml/2 tbsp vinegar

salt and Szechuan pepper

---

1 Marinate the meat with the juniper berries, sesame oil, soy sauce, Hoisin sauce and five-spice powder for 2 hours.
2 Heat the groundnut oil in a wok. Add the meat and stir-fry for 8 minutes until cooked. Remove the meat from the wok.
3 Add the spring onions and mushrooms to the wok and stir-fry for 3 minutes, stirring continuously.
4 Return the meat to the pan, then mix in the honey and vinegar. Season to taste with salt and pepper and reheat, stirring.

Photograph opposite (top)

23

Fried Pork with Chutney

Serves 4
Preparation time: 30 mins
3340 kcal/14030 kJ

5 ml/1 tsp five-spice powder
5 ml/1 tsp curry powder
500 g/1 1/4 lb belly of pork, cut into narrow strips
30 ml/2 tbsp groundnut oil
1 bunch spring onions, cut into strips
1 stalk celery, cut into strips
100 g/4 oz beansprouts
1 x 200 g/7 oz/jar Chinese sweet pickles, diced
45 ml/3 tbsp mango chutney
30 ml/2 tbsp soy sauce
30 ml/2 tbsp tomato purée
150 ml/1/4 pt/2/3 cup chicken stock
10 ml/2 tsp cornflour mixed with 15 ml/1 tbsp water
salt and pepper

1 Rub the spices well into the pork. Heat the oil in a wok and stir-fry the meat for 8 to 10 minutes until cooked. Remove the meat from the wok.
2 Add the vegetables to the wok and fry, stirring continuously, for 5 minutes. Return the pork to the pan with all the remaining ingredients except the cornflour and water. Heat throughout.
3 Add the cornflour and water and continue to stir-fry until boiling. Simmer gently for 2 minutes.

Photograph opposite (top)

Turkey with Peppers

Serves 4
Preparation time: 30 mins
1320 kcal/5540 kJ

30 ml/2 tbsp groundnut oil
1 medium Chinese cabbage, cut into strips
350 g/12 oz smoked turkey ham, cut into strips
1 onion, sliced
1 red pepper, cut into strips
1 green pepper, cut into strips
4 Chinese mushrooms, soaked and cut into strips
120 ml/4 fl oz/1/2 cup chicken stock
30 ml/2 tbsp tomato purée
45 ml/3 tbsp vinegar
30 ml/2 tbsp soy sauce
15 ml/1 tbsp Hoisin sauce
10 ml/2 tsp cornflour mixed with 15 ml/1 tbsp water
salt and pepper
a few drops of chilli oil

1 Heat half the oil in a wok and stir-fry the cabbage for 3 to 5 minutes or until cooked down. Remove the cabbage from the wok.
2 Add the turkey breast or ham to the wok and stir-fry quickly for 1 minute.
3 Add the vegetables stir-fry for 3 to 4 minutes.
4 Mix the chicken stock with the tomato purée, vinegar and sauces and add to the vegetables. Return the cabbage to the wok. Stir in the cornflour and water and bring just up to the boil. Season.

Photograph opposite (bottom left)

Fried Chicken and Broccoli

Serves 4
Preparation time: 35 mins
3380 kcal/14220 kJ

450 g/1 lb chicken meat, chopped into 4 cm/1 1/2 in pieces
225 g/8 oz chicken livers
45 ml/3 tbsp flour, seasoned with salt and pepper
45 ml/3 tbsp groundnut oil
1 onion, diced
1 red pepper, diced
1 green pepper, diced
225 g/8 oz broccoli florets
4 slices fresh or tinned pineapple, diced
30 ml/2 tbsp tomato purée
30 ml/2 tbsp Hoisin sauce
30 ml/2 tbsp honey
30 ml/2 tbsp soy sauce
300 ml/1/2 pt/1 1/4 cups chicken stock
10 ml/2 tsp sesame oil

1 Toss the chicken and chicken livers in the flour.
2 Heat the groundnut oil in a wok and stir-fry the liver for 5 minutes. Remove the liver.
3 Add the chicken pieces to the wok, cover and fry over a moderate heat for 20 minutes, stirring occasionally.
4 Add the vegetables and pineapple and stir-fry for 10 minutes. Return the livers to the wok, add the remaining ingredients and bring to the boil.

Photograph opposite (bottom right)

Crisply-Fried Specialities

This chapter contains a range of classic Chinese dishes, some wrapped in pastry, others cloaked with crumbs, all fried to a delicious crispness and absolutely delicious. It also includes recipes for other Oriental specialities such as tasty spare ribs.

Piquant Spring Rolls, page 28

27

Lamb with Mange-Tout

Serves 4
Preparation time: 25 mins
1390 kcal/5840 kJ

2 cloves garlic
salt and pepper
450 g/1 lb leg of lamb, diced
30-45 ml/2-3 tbsp cornflour
30 ml/2 tbsp groundnut oil
450 g/1 lb mange-tout, each cut into 4 pieces
250 ml/8 fl oz/1 cup chicken stock
10 ml/2 tsp grated lemon rind
30 ml/2 tbsp honey
30 ml/2 tbsp soy sauce
5 ml/1 tsp coriander seeds, coarsely ground
5 ml/1 tsp caraway seeds, coarsely ground
5 ml/1 tsp aniseed, coarsely ground
30 ml/2 tbsp tomato purée
30 ml/2 tbsp vinegar

1 Crush the garlic with the salt. Season the lamb, then toss in the garlic.
2 Coat the pieces of meat in cornflour. Heat the oil in a wok, add the lamb and stir-fry until cooked.
3 Add the mange-tout and stir-fry for 2 minutes.
4 Mix the remaining cornflour with the stock. Pour into the wok and add the remaining ingredients. Bring to the boil, stirring, simmer for 2 minutes and season.

Photograph opposite (top)

Piquant Spring Rolls

Serves 4
Preparation time: 1 hour
3100 kcal/13020 kJ

8 spring roll pastry wrappers (sold frozen in Oriental supermarkets)
1/2 bunch spring onions, finely chopped
1 x 200 g/7 oz/small tin beansprouts, drained
225 g/8 oz cooked ham, cut into very thin strips
30 ml/2 tbsp tomato purée
45 ml/3 tbsp soy sauce
15 ml/1 tbsp honey
30 ml/2 tbsp cornflour
5 ml/1 tsp five-spice powder
salt and pepper
oil for frying

1 Arrange 1 wrapper at a time on a work surface. Mix together all the filling ingredients and season to taste with salt and pepper. Divide into 8 portions.
2 Place one portion of filling near the point of one wrapper. Fold the pastry over the filling like an envelope, then moisten the edges and roll up. Repeat with the remaining filling and wrappers.
3 Heat the oil in the wok for deep-frying and fry the spring rolls until golden brown and crisp. Remove from the wok and drain thoroughly before serving.

Photograph page 26

Deep-Fried Spare Ribs

Serves 4
Preparation time: 1 1/4 hours
3040 kcal/12770 kJ

2 kg/4 1/2 lb spare ribs, cut into 5 cm/2 in pieces
salt
Szechuan pepper
Marinade:
120 ml/4 fl oz/1/2 cup tomato ketchup
120 ml/4 fl oz/1/2 cup vinegar
60 ml/4 tbsp mango chutney
45 ml/3 tbsp medium sherry or Chinese rice wine
2 cloves garlic, chopped
5 ml/1 tsp salt
45 ml/3 tbsp soy sauce
30 ml/2 tbsp honey
15 ml/1 tbsp mild curry powder
15 ml/1 tbsp paprika
oil for frying
60 ml/4 tbsp chopped chives

1 Season the spare ribs with salt and pepper. Mix together all the marinade ingredients. Pour over the spare ribs and marinate for at least 1 hour in a covered dish.
2 Heat the oil in the wok and fry the ribs until crisp. Remove and serve sprinkled with chives.

Photograph opposite (bottom)

Dough Pockets with Meat Filling

Serves 4
Preparation time: 1¹/₂ hours
3300 kcal/13860 kJ

Dough:

450 g/1 lb strong plain white flour
1 sachet easy-mix yeast
10 ml/2 tsp caster sugar
5 ml/1 tsp salt
300 ml/¹/₂ pt/1¹/₄ cups warm milk or water

Filling:

225 g/8 oz pork or turkey breast fillet, minced
225 g/8 oz fresh or tinned crab meat, minced
1 onion, finely chopped
30 ml/2 tbsp soy sauce
30 ml/2 tbsp oyster sauce
1 egg, beaten
15 ml/1 tbsp cornflour
salt and Szechuan pepper

1 Sieve the flour into a bowl. Add the remaining dough ingredients and knead well to a workable and elastic mixture. Cover and leave to rise in a warm place for 45 minutes.
2 Knead the dough again, then divide into 8. Roll into 20 cm/8 in squares.
3 Mix the filling ingredients and season. Pile the filling equally over the dough pieces, brush the edges with water and fold into triangles.
4 Heat some oil in a wok and deep-fry until golden.

Photograph (left)

Crispy-Fried Spiced Chicken

Serves 4
Preparation time: 40 mins
2860 kcal/12010 kJ

*1 x 2 kg/**4 lb** chicken*
salt and Szechuan pepper
Marinade:
*30 ml/**2 tbsp** soy sauce*
*30 ml/**2 tbsp** plum sauce*
*45 ml/**3 tbsp** mango chutney*
1 clove garlic, chopped
*2.5 ml/¹/₂ **tsp** ginger*
a few drops of brandy

*30-45 ml/**2-3 tbsp** cornflour*
2 eggs, beaten
*100 g/**4 oz**/1 cup dried breadcrumbs*
*30 ml/**2 tbsp** groundnut oil*
1 bunch spring onions, chopped
1 red pepper, diced
1 green pepper, diced
*30 ml/**2 tbsp** soy sauce*
*30 ml/**2 tbsp** honey*
*30 ml/**2 tbsp** vinegar*

1 Chop the chicken into 5 cm/2 in pieces. Season. Mix the marinade ingredients and marinate the chicken for 2 hours.
2 Drain the chicken. Dust with cornflour, then toss in eggs and breadcrumbs.
3 Fry the chicken in hot oil, then remove. Stir-fry the vegetables for 5 minutes, then remove.
4 Drain the wok, add all the ingredients and heat until boiling.

Photograph (right)

Shrimp Balls

Hot Diced Fish

Serves 4
Preparation time: 30 mins
1210 kcal/5080 kJ

---

500 g/1 1/4 lb prawns, weight before shelling

150 g/5 oz belly of pork, cubed

1 onion

1 sprig parsley

1 sprig dill

1 egg, beaten

30 ml/2 tbsp oyster sauce

15 ml/1 tbsp soy sauce

salt

Szechuan pepper

a few drops of lemon juice

a pinch of brown sugar

30-45 ml/2-3 tbsp cornflour

oil for frying

---

1 Put the prawns, pork, onion and herbs through a mincer, using the fine blade.
2 Mix with the egg, oyster sauce and soy sauce until smooth. Season with salt, pepper, lemon juice and sugar and bind to a firm mixture with the cornflour.
3 With wet hands, make into small balls and deep fry in sizzling oil for about 5 to 7 minutes until cooked through.

Photograph opposite (top)

Serves 4
Preparation time: 30 mins
1140 kcal/4790 kJ

---

600 g/1 1/2 lb haddock or hake fillet, diced

juice of 1 lemon

Marinade:

30 ml/2 tbsp soy sauce

30 ml/2 tbsp oyster sauce

15 ml/1 tbsp grated lemon rind

a pinch of powdered ginger

salt

Szechuan pepper

2 egg whites

30-45 ml/2-3 tbsp cornflour

---

oil for frying

1 bunch spring onions, cut into fine strips

1 stalk celery, cut into strips

6 Chinese mushrooms, soaked and cut into strips

100 g/4 oz bamboo shoots, cut into strips

250 ml/8 fl oz/1 cup chicken stock

5 ml/1 tsp cornflour

5 ml/1 tsp five-spice powder

5 ml/1 tsp Szechuan pepper, coarsely ground

---

1 Put the diced fish into a bowl and sprinkle with the lemon juice. Mix together the marinade ingredients, add to the fish, cover and marinate for 1 1/2 hours.

2 Heat the oil in a wok until sizzling and fry the diced fish briefly until cooked. Remove the fish from the wok and keep it warm.
3 Add the vegetables to the remaining oil and deep-fry. Carefully pour off the oil. Mix the chicken stock with the cornflour, add to the vegetables and bring to the boil.
4 Return the fish to the wok, reheat quickly, season to taste with five-spice powder and pepper and serve immediately.

Photograph opposite (bottom)

Variation
A sweet and sour variation of this dish can be made by using fruit instead of vegetables. Stir-fry 2 diced peppers, 1 finely diced onion, 4 finely cut pineapple slices and 100 g/4 oz lychees in the remaining oil. Thin down with 60 ml/4 tbsp tomato ketchup and 60 ml/4 tbsp dry sherry, as well as 30 ml/2 tbsp honey and 30 ml/2 tbsp vinegar. Season to taste with curry powder, pepper and salt. The dish can also be sprinkled with finely chopped chives.

33

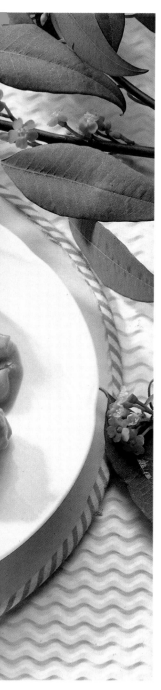

Sweet and Sour Pork

Serves 4
Preparation time: 40 mins
plus marinating
2920 kcal/12260 kJ

---

500 g/1 1/4 lb pork fillet,
diced

---

30 ml/2 **tbsp** soy sauce

---

30 ml/2 **tbsp** plum sauce

---

salt

Szechuan pepper, coarsely
ground

Batter:

---

225 g/8 **oz** plain flour

---

250 ml/8 fl **oz**/1 cup dry
white wine

---

2 eggs, separated

---

oil for frying

---

1 onion, diced

---

1 red pepper, diced

---

1 green pepper, diced

---

2 slices pineapple, diced

---

60 ml/4 **tbsp** tomato ketchup

---

15 ml/1 **tbsp** cornflour
smoothly mixed with
120 ml/4 fl **oz**/1/2 cup cold
water

---

45 ml/3 **tbsp** honey

---

60 ml/4 **tbsp** vinegar

---

1 Wash the pork under running water, pat dry and put into a bowl. Stir the soy and plum sauces together and mix with the meat. Season the meat well with salt and Szechuan pepper and marinate for at least 2 hours in a covered dish in the refrigerator. Drain.

2 For the batter, smoothly beat the flour with the wine and the egg yolks in a bowl. Whisk the egg whites until very stiff and carefully fold into the batter. Turn the marinated pork in the mixture.

3 Heat the oil in a wok until sizzling. Deep-fry the diced pork until golden. Remove the meat from the wok and keep it warm.

4 Add the vegetables to the fat and deep-fry. Remove from the wok.

5 Pour off the fat. Add the pineapple to the wok, then return the pork and vegetables to the pan. Heat through, stirring continuously.

6 Mix the tomato ketchup with the cornflour mixture, honey and vinegar. Season with salt and pepper. Pour into wok and bring the ingredients to the boil, stirring continuously. Simmer for 1 1/2 minutes.

Stuffed Courgette Bites

Serves 4
Preparation time: 30 mins
1530 kcal/6420 kJ

---

4 medium to large courgettes

225 g/8 oz pork, minced

225 g/8 oz crab meat, finely minced

2 eggs, beaten

30 ml/2 tbsp soy sauce

30 ml/2 tbsp oyster sauce

a pinch of powdered ginger

salt and pepper

75 ml/5 tbsp cornflour

50 g/2 oz soft breadcrumbs

oil for frying

---

1 Clean the courgettes, cut in half lengthways and remove the seeds and cores with a teaspoon.
2 Mix the pork with the crab meat, eggs and sauces until smooth. Season with ginger, salt and pepper and bind with cornflour and breadcrumbs. Cover and put into freezer for 30 minutes.
3 Fill the courgettes with the mixture, cut them into 5 cm/2 in slices. Heat the oil in a wok and deep-fry the courgettes until golden. Remove, drain and serve.

Photograph opposite (centre)

Vegetable Surprises

Serves 4
Preparation time: 25 mins
plus marinating
1570 kcal/6590 kJ

---

225 g/8 oz broccoli florets

225 g/8 oz cauliflower florets

225 g/8 oz Brussels sprouts

30 ml/2 tbsp honey

30 ml/2 tbsp soy sauce

30 ml/2 tbsp vinegar

5 ml/1 tsp five-spice powder

salt and pepper

Batter:

225 g/8 oz flour

250 ml/8 fl oz/1 cup dry white wine

2 eggs, separated

a pinch of salt

15 ml/1 tbsp grated lemon rind

oil for frying

---

1 Blanch the vegetables in boiling water and drain.
2 Mix together the honey, soy sauce, vinegar and five-spice powder and season with salt and pepper. Place the vegetables in this marinade, cover and marinate in the refrigerator for 2 hours.
3 Mix the flour, wine and egg yolks until smooth. Whip the egg whites until stiff, then fold them into the batter. Season with salt, pepper and lemon rind.
4 Drain the vegetables and coat them in the batter. Heat the oil and deep-fry until golden.

Photograph opposite (bottom)

Deep-Fried Meatballs

Serves 4
Preparation time: 25 mins
1810 kcal/7600 kJ

---

450 g/1 lb lean ground beef

1 onion, finely chopped

4 Chinese mushrooms, soaked and finely chopped

1 egg, beaten

30 ml/2 tbsp finely chopped chives

5 ml/1 tsp five-spice powder

2 cloves garlic, crushed

salt and Szechuan pepper

oil for frying

30 ml/2 tbsp soy sauce

30 ml/2 tbsp medium sherry

30 ml/2 tbsp Hoisin sauce

---

1 Mix together the beef, onion, mushrooms, egg, chives, five-spice powder and garlic. Season to taste with salt and pepper. With floured hands, shape the mixture into small balls.
2 Heat the oil in a wok and deep-fry the meatballs until golden.
3 Mix together the soy sauce, sherry and Hoisin sauce. Drain the meatballs and serve straight away accompanied by the bowl of sauce.

Photograph opposite (top)

Golden Coins

Serves 4
Preparation time: 50 mins
plus marinating
1530 kcal/6420 kJ

4 chicken breast fillets
30 ml/2 **tbsp** honey
30 ml/2 **tbsp** vinegar
30 ml/2 **tbsp** tomato ketchup
30 ml/2 **tbsp** soy sauce
a pinch of salt
2 cloves garlic, crushed
5 ml/1 **tsp** five-spice powder
30-45 ml/**2-3 tbsp** plain flour
2 eggs, beaten
5 ml/1 **tsp** grated fresh root ginger
5 ml/1 **tsp** grated lemon rind
100 g/4 **oz**/1 cup dried breadcrumbs
oil for frying

1 Put the chicken in a bowl. Mix together the honey, vinegar, tomato ketchup, soy sauce, salt, garlic and five-spice powder. Pour over the chicken, cover and marinate in the refrigerator for 12 hours.
2 Remove the chicken from the marinade and cut it into finger-thick strips. Dust with flour.
3 Lightly beat the eggs with the ginger and lemon rind. Coat the chicken with the mixture, then toss them in the breadcrumbs until evenly coated.
4 Heat the oil in a wok and deep-fry the chicken until golden brown.

Photograph opposite (top left)

Drunken Chicken

Serves 4
Preparation time: 40 mins
plus marinating
1910 kcal/8020 kJ

1 x 2 kg/**4 lb** roasting chicken, skinned
60 ml/**4 tbsp** soy sauce
30 ml/2 **tbsp** Hoisin sauce
30 ml/2 **tbsp** plum sauce
30 ml/2 **tbsp** vinegar
2 cloves garlic, crushed
salt
a few drops of chilli oil
2 egg whites
60 ml/**4 tbsp** cornflour
oil for frying
300 ml/¹/₂ **pt**/1 ¹/₄ cups dry sherry or Chinese rice wine

1 Chop the chicken into 5 cm/2 in pieces and put it in a bowl. Beat together the sauces, vinegar, garlic, salt and chilli oil. Pour over the chicken, cover and marinate in the refrigerator for 4 hours.
2 Beat the egg whites until stiff, then fold in the cornflour. Remove the chicken from the marinade and coat with the egg white mixture.
3 Heat the oil in a wok and deep-fry the chicken until cooked through and golden brown. Drain well and put into a bowl. Pour over the sherry or rice wine, then cover and leave to marinate in the refrigerator for 12 hours. Remove the chicken from the wine and serve cold.

Photograph opposite (top right)

Fried Meat Kebabs

Serves 4
Preparation time: 40 mins
plus marinating
1790 kcal/7520 kJ

450 g/**1 lb** pork fillet, thinly sliced
100 g/4 **oz** cooked ham, thinly sliced
6 water chestnuts, thinly sliced
30 ml/2 **tbsp** soy sauce
30 ml/2 **tbsp** vinegar
15 ml/1 **tbsp** brown sugar
15 ml/1 **tbsp** oyster sauce
a few drops of chilli oil
45 ml/3 **tbsp** cornflour
30 ml/3 **tbsp** sherry
2-3 eggs, beaten
oil for frying

1 Thread the pork fillet, ham and water chestnuts alternately on to small skewers.
2 Mix together the soy sauce, vinegar, sugar, oyster sauce and chilli oil. Place the kebabs in this marinade, cover and marinate in the refrigerator for 3 hours.
3 Mix the cornflour, sherry and eggs to a smooth, thickish batter. Twist the kebabs in the batter to coat them.
4 Heat the oil in a wok and deep-fry the kebabs until light golden brown.

Photograph opposite (bottom)

Boiled and Braised in the Wok

This section proves the versatility of the wok and offers a tempting gathering of simmered and braised dishes plus an ingenious beef soup which is perfect for cold winter days.

Piquant Beef Soup, page 42

Piquant Beef Soup

Serves 4
Preparation time: 30 mins
1580 kcal/6640 kJ

1 clove garlic, crushed

salt

45 ml/3 tbsp groundnut oil

225 g/8 oz ground beef

1 bunch spring onions, cut into strips

1 red pepper, cut into strips

1 green pepper, cut into strips

225 g/8 oz green cabbage, cut into strips

1 l/1¾ pts/4¼ cups chicken or beef stock

30 ml/2 tbsp plum sauce

30 ml/2 tbsp Hoisin sauce

45 ml/3 tbsp soy sauce

2 pieces stem ginger in syrup, chopped

2 eggs

5 ml/1 tsp sesame oil

Szechuan pepper

225 g/8 oz clear or glass noodles, soaked

1 Mix the garlic and salt. Heat with the groundnut oil and the meat and brown quickly, stirring.
2 Add the vegetables and sweat, stirring, until glassy.
3 Add the stock, plum and Hoisin sauces, 30 ml/2 tbsp soy sauce and the ginger. Cook for 10 minutes.
4 Beat the eggs with the soy sauce, sesame oil and pepper. Add to the soup with the noodles. Cook until the eggs form strands and the noodles are tender. Season.
Photograph page 40

Duck with Vegetables

Serves 4
Preparation time: 90 mins
3090 kcal/12980 kJ

1 large prepared duck, chopped into 16 pieces

salt

300 ml/½ pt/1¼ cups dry white wine

120 ml/4 fl oz/½ cup vinegar

Szechuan pepper, coarsely ground

45 ml/3 tbsp soy sauce

30 ml/2 tbsp plum sauce

30 ml/2 tbsp Hoisin sauce

5 ml/1 tsp five-spice powder

1 bunch spring onions, chopped

2 carrots, finely chopped

1 x 5 cm/2 in white radish (rettich), chopped

1 Chinese cabbage, diced

5 ml/1 tsp sugar

chopped fresh herbs

1 Put the duck pieces into a wok and cover with salt water. Add the wine, vinegar, sauces and spices, cover and simmer for about 70 minutes.
2 Add the vegetables to the meat 10 minutes before the end of cooking time.
3 Season well with salt, pepper and sugar, then cool. Cover and refrigerate overnight. Skim off fat, then reheat the duck in its own liquid for 20 minutes. Serve sprinkled with herbs.
Photograph opposite (top)

Vegetables in Tomato Sauce

Serves 4
Preparation time: 40 mins
1410 kcal/5920 kJ

salt

2 cloves garlic, crushed

30 ml/2 tbsp groundnut oil

100 g/4 oz smoked bacon, diced

30 ml/2 tbsp tomato purée

30 ml/2 tbsp soy sauce

30 ml/2 tbsp honey

30 ml/2 tbsp Hoisin sauce

300 ml/½ pt/1¼ cups vegetable stock

1 red pepper, cut into strips

1 green pepper, cut into strips

1 stalk celery, cut into strips

100 g/4 oz beansprouts

100 g/4 oz green peas

10 ml/2 tsp vinegar

1 Mix the garlic cloves with the salt and put in the wok with the oil and bacon. Fry until the bacon is crisp but still pale.
2 Mix together the tomato purée, soy sauce, honey and hoisin sauce, then blend in the stock.
3 Add the vegetables and vinegar, then pour the mixture into the wok, cover and braise until cooked.

Photograph opposite (bottom)

43

Seafood in Stock

Serves 4
Preparation time: 40 mins
1770 kcal/7430 kJ

1 clove garlic
salt
45 ml/**3 tbsp** groundnut oil
2 carrots, chopped
1 stalk celery, sliced
5 ml/**1 tsp** cloves
5 ml/**1 tsp** juniper berries
5 ml/**1 tsp** red peppercorns
5 ml/**1 tsp** coriander
5 ml/**1 tsp** pimento
300 ml/$^1/_2$ **pt**/1 $^1/_4$ cups dry white wine
1 l/1$^3/_4$ **pts**/4 $^1/_4$ cups vegetable stock
120 ml/**4 fl oz**/$^1/_2$ cup vinegar
60 ml/**4 tbsp** soy sauce
45 ml/**3 tbsp** oyster sauce
8 large prawns
450 g/**1 lb** mussels
225 g/**8 oz** squid rings, blanched
50 g/**2 oz** dried fish (from Oriental stores)
Szechuan pepper

1 Crush the garlic clove with the salt and heat in the wok with the oil, vegetables and spices.
2 Add the wine, stock, vinegar, soy and oyster sauces, then bring to the boil. Lower the heat.
3 Add the seafood and dried fish, then leave to bubble over a medium heat for 20 minutes. Season well again and serve in bowls.

Photograph (top)

Braised Fish

Serves 4
Preparation time: 35 mins
1420 kcal/5969 kJ

1 clove garlic	
salt	
30 ml/**2 tbsp** groundnut oil	
1 onion, chopped	
1 green pepper, chopped	
100 g/**4 oz** fresh beansprouts	
6 Chinese mushrooms, soaked and cut into strips	
50 ml/**2 fl oz**/¹/₄ cup tomato ketchup	
10 ml/**2 tbsp** cornflour mixed with 15 ml/**1 tbsp** water	
30 ml/**2 tbsp** honey	
30 ml/**2 tbsp** vinegar	
30 ml/**2 tbsp** soy sauce	
45 ml/**3 tbsp** mango chutney	
450 g/**1 lb** fish fillets, such as haddock or plaice, diced	
juice of 1 lemon	
5 ml/**1 tsp** five-spice powder	
salt and Szechuan pepper	

1 Crush the garlic clove with the salt. Heat the oil in a wok and stir-fry the garlic and the prepared vegetables until tender but still crisp.
2 Add the tomato ketchup, cornflour mixture, honey, vinegar, soy sauce and chutney. Bring slowly to a gentle boil and simmer for 2 minutes.
3 Sprinkle the fish fillets with the lemon juice and season with the five-spice powder. Add to the vegetables, braise for 5 to 7 minutes and season to taste with salt and pepper.

Photograph (bottom)

Spicy Braised Pork

Serves 4
Preparation time: 2 hours
3470 kcal/14575 kJ

---

600 g/1 1/2 lb belly of pork,
diced

salt and Szechuan pepper

5 ml/1 tsp black pepper

30 ml/2 tbsp soy sauce

30 ml/2 tbsp Hoisin sauce

45 ml/3 tbsp groundnut oil

120 ml/4 fl oz/1/2 cup rice
wine or dry sherry

300 ml/1/2 pt/1 1/4 cups
chicken stock

5 ml/1 tsp five-spice powder

1 bunch spring onions,
chopped

225 g/8 oz oyster
mushrooms, cleaned and
sliced

15 ml/1 tbsp cornflour mixed
with 30 ml/2 tbsp water

---

1 Season the meat well
with salt, Szechuan pep-
per and black pepper.
Marinate in a covered dish
with the sauces for 1 hour.
2 Heat the oil in a wok and
stir-fry the meat until
golden brown. Add the
rice wine or sherry, stock
and five-spice powder.
Cover and simmer over a
moderate heat for 1 hour.
3 Add the spring onions
and oyster mushrooms
and continue to simmer,
uncovered, for 3 minutes.
Blend in the cornflour and
water and bring mixture to
the boil, stirring. Simmer
for 2 minutes.

*Photograph opposite
(top)*

Braised Pork Knuckle in Red Sauce

Serves 4
Preparation   time: 1 1/2
hours
3340 kcal/14030 kJ

---

1 large knuckle of pork

1 l/1 3/4 pts/4 1/4 cups boiling
water

salt

120 ml/4 fl oz/1/2 cup
vinegar

45 ml/3 tbsp soy sauce

45 ml/3 tbsp honey

5 ml/1 tsp juniper berries

5 ml/1 tsp aniseed

5 ml/1 tsp coriander

Szechuan pepper

60 ml/4 tbsp groundnut oil

1 bunch spring onions,
sliced

2 carrots, thinly sliced

1 stalk celery, sliced

60 ml/4 tbsp soy sauce

45 ml/3 tbsp Hoisin sauce

30 ml/2 tbsp mango chutney

75 ml/5 tbsp tomato ketchup

1 clove garlic, crushed

60 ml/4 tbsp chopped
chives

---

1 Bring the knuckle of
pork to the boil in a wok
with the water, salt, vinegar, soy sauce, honey,
spices and pepper. Add
the prepared vegetables.
Bring back to the boil,
lower the heat and cover.
Simmer for about 1 1/4 to 1
1/2 hours until tender.

2 Remove the meat from
the wok, cut the meat off
the bone and dice it. Heat
the oil in a wok and fry the
meat,   stirring   continuously, until golden brown.
Add the vegetables and
stir-fry   together   for   5
minutes.
3 Add   the   sauces,
chutney, tomato ketchup
and garlic. Bring to the
boil, stirring continuously,
and simmer for 2 minutes.
Season to taste with salt
and pepper and serve
sprinkled with chives.

*Photograph opposite
(bottom)*

Variation
Why not try the following
cooking   method.   After
boiling, brown the knuckle
of pork on all sides in the
groundnut oil, sprinkling
with   soy   sauce   while
browning.   Next   add
300   ml/1/2   pt/1 1/4   cups
chicken stock, 2 crushed
cloves garlic and some
vegetables (2 onions, 2
carrots, 1 leek, 1 stalk of
celery, all cut into strips).
Season with 30 ml/2 tbsp
vinegar and plum sauce,
salt and pepper, and
leave to braise again for
10 to 15 minutes. Corn-
flour can be used if you
wish to thicken the sauce.

47

Braised Beef with Mushrooms

Serves 4
Preparation time: 1½ hours plus marinating
3460 kcal/14530 kJ

---

1 kg/2 lb topside of beef

---

salt

Szechuan pepper

Marinade:

---

60 ml/4 tbsp soy sauce

---

30 ml/2 tbsp Hoisin sauce

---

30 ml/2 tbsp honey

---

30 ml/2 tbsp vinegar

---

5 ml/1 tsp peppercorns, coarsely ground

---

5 ml/1 tsp aniseed, coarsely ground

---

5 ml/1 tsp coriander, coarsely ground

---

60 ml/4 tbsp groundnut oil

---

5 ml/2 tsp cornflour smoothly mixed with 15 ml/1 tbsp cold water

---

1 x 400 g/14 oz/large tin peeled tomatoes

---

1 bunch spring onions, cut into strips

---

6 Chinese mushrooms, soaked and cut into strips

---

2 carrots, coarsely grated

---

30 ml/2 tbsp plum sauce

---

60 ml/4 tbsp chopped chives

---

1 Rinse the prepared joint of beef under running water. Pat dry and pierce several times with a fork. Season with salt and pepper and place in a dish.

2 Mix the marinade ingredients together well, pour over the meat, cover and leave to marinate in the refrigerator overnight.

3 Heat the oil in a wok. Add the meat and sizzle until well browned, turning frequently.

4 Add the cornflour mixture and tomatoes. Braise the beef over a moderate heat for 1¼ to 1½ hours or until tender.

5 Add the vegetables 10 minutes before the end of cooking time and cook until tender but still firm.

6 Add the plum sauce, then adjust the seasoning to taste.

7 Remove the meat from the sauce and cut into bite-sized pieces. Return the meat to the sauce, reheat and serve sprinkled with chives.

Braised Duck with Green Beans

Serves 4
Preparation time: 1½ hours plus marinating
3940 kcal/16550 kJ

---
1 oven-ready duck
---
60 ml/*4 tbsp* groundnut oil
---
2 cloves garlic, crushed
---
salt
---
1 onion, chopped
---
15 ml/*1 tbsp* freshly grated root ginger
---
45 ml/*3 tbsp* soy sauce
---
120 ml/*4 fl oz*/½ cup rice wine or dry sherry
---
60 ml/*4 tbsp* tomato ketchup
---
45 ml/*3 tbsp* vinegar
---
300 ml/½ *pt*/1¼ cups chicken stock
---
450 g/1 *lb* green beans, cleaned and sliced
---
freshly ground pepper
---
5 or 6 drops chilli oil
---
15 ml/*1 tbsp* cornflour mixed with 30 ml/*2 tbsp* water
---

1 Chop duck into 8 or 10 pieces. Heat oil and stir-fry the duck until golden brown. Transfer to a bowl.
2 Add garlic to the bowl with the salt, onion, ginger, soy sauce, wine or sherry, ketchup and vinegar. Mix, cover and marinate in refrigerator for 3 hours.
3 Reheat oil. Add duck, stock and marinade. Bring to the boil, cover and simmer for 1 hour.
4 Add the beans, cover and simmer for 15 minutes. Season, add the chilli oil and cornflour, bring to the boil, stirring, and simmer for 2 minutes.
Photograph opposite (top)

Far Eastern Chicken

Serves 4
Preparation time: 50 mins
3540 kcal/14870 kJ

---
1 oven-ready chicken
---
60 ml/*4 tbsp* groundnut oil
---
2 cloves garlic
---
salt
---
2 onions, chopped
---
2 pieces stem ginger in syrup, chopped
---
45 ml/*3 tbsp* soy sauce
---
30 ml/*2 tbsp* Hoisin sauce
---
50 ml/*2 fl oz*/¼ cup Chinese rice wine or dry sherry
---
300 ml/½ *pt*/⅔ cup chicken stock
---
5 ml/*1 tsp* pepper
---
6 hard-boiled eggs, chopped
---
15 ml/*1 tbsp* cornflour mixed with 15 ml/*1 tbsp* water
---
freshly ground pepper
---

1 Chop the chicken into 5 cm/2 in pieces.
2 Heat the oil in a wok, add the chicken and fry over a moderate heat until golden brown, stirring.
3 Crush the garlic with the salt and add with the onions and ginger. Quickly fry together.
4 Add the sauces, rice wine or sherry, stock and pepper, then cover and braise over a moderate heat for 30 minutes until cooked.
5 Fold in the eggs, stir in the cornflour, then bring up to the boil. Simmer for 1 minute, stirring.

Photograph opposite (centre)

Braised Chicken with Eggs

Serves 4
Preparation time: 50 mins
1970 kcal/8270 kJ

---
30 ml/*2 tbsp* groundnut oil
---
4 chicken breast fillets, cut into strips
---
1 red pepper, cut into strips
---
1 green pepper, cut into strips
---
45 ml/*3 tbsp* soy sauce
---
50 ml/*2 fl oz*/¼ cup dry white wine
---
250 ml/*8 fl oz*/1 cup chicken stock
---
100 g/*4 oz* iceberg lettuce, shredded
---
salt and pepper
---
5 ml/*1 tsp* brown sugar
---
30 ml/*2 tbsp* Hoisin sauce
---
15 ml/*1 tbsp* cornflour mixed with 15 ml/*1 tbsp* water
---
4 eggs
---
30 ml/*2 tbsp* sherry
---

1 Heat the oil in a wok and quickly brown the chicken and peppers, stirring. Pour in the soy sauce, wine and stock. Cover and simmer for 30 minutes.
2 Mix in the lettuce, season with salt, pepper, sugar and Hoisin sauce. Add the cornflour and bring to the boil, stirring.
3 Beat the eggs with the sherry and fry as thin omelettes. Sprinkle with salt and pepper, tear into pieces and arrange in a serving dish. Spoon the chicken mixture on top.

Photograph opposite (bottom)

Prawns with Vegetables

Serves 4
Preparation time: 30 mins
plus marinating
1320 kcal/5545 kJ

450 g/1 lb shelled prawns
45 ml/3 tbsp soy sauce
30 ml/2 tbsp oyster sauce
60 ml/4 tbsp Chinese rice wine or dry sherry
juice of 1 lemon
60 ml/4 tbsp groundnut oil
1 bunch spring onions, cut into strips
2 carrots, cut into strips
1 stalk celery, cut into strips
4 Chinese mushrooms, soaked and cut into strips
100 g/4 oz beansprouts
300 ml/1/2 pt/1 1/4 cups chicken stock
5 ml/1 tsp curry powder
5 ml/1 tsp paprika
salt and pepper
20 ml/4 tsp cornflour mixed with 15 ml/1 tbsp water

1 Marinate the prawns with the sauces, wine or sherry and lemon juice, for 2 hours.
2 Heat the oil in a wok, add the vegetables and stir-fry for 5 minutes.
3 Add the prawns and stock. Bring to the boil and cover. Braise for 10 minutes until cooked. Season to taste with curry powder, paprika, salt and pepper. Add the cornflour and bring to the boil. Simmer for 1 minute.

Photograph (top)

Beef in Red Sauce

Serves 4
Preparation time: 40 mins
2960 kcal/12430 kJ

*60 ml/**4 tbsp** groundnut oil*
*450 g/**1 lb** ground beef*
1 onion, finely chopped
1 red pepper, finely chopped
1 green pepper, finely chopped
2 slices canned pineapple, finely chopped
*45 ml/**3 tbsp** soy sauce*
*50 ml/**2 fl oz**/¹/₄ cup dry white wine*
*30 ml/**2 tbsp** vinegar*
*30 ml/**2 tbsp** honey*
*300 ml/¹/₂ **pt**/1¹/₄ cups chicken or beef stock*
salt
freshly ground pepper
a few drops of chilli oil

1 Heat the oil in a wok, add the beef and brown over a fairly brisk heat, stir-frying continuously.
2 Add the vegetables and pineapple and stir-fry quickly for 3 minutes. Add the soy sauce, wine, vinegar, honey and stock.
3 Bring to the boil, lower the heat and cover. Simmer over a medium heat for 30 minutes until cooked. Season to taste with salt, pepper and chilli oil.

Photograph (bottom)

Pork with Mushrooms

Serves 4
Preparation time: 1 hour
plus marinating
2340 kcal/9830 kJ

---

450 g/1 lb pork, diced

45 ml/3 tbsp soy sauce

45 ml/3 tbsp tomato ketchup

45 ml/3 tbsp dry sherry or
dry white wine

5 ml/1 tsp five-spice powder

15 ml/1 tbsp brown sugar

30 ml/2 tbsp groundnut oil

1 onion, chopped

6 Chinese mushrooms,
soaked and cut into strips

2 red peppers, chopped

300 ml/1/2 pt/1 1/4 cups
chicken or beef stock

salt and pepper

a few drops of chilli oil

15 ml/1 tbsp cornflour mixed
with 15 ml/1 tbsp water

---

1 Combine the pork with
the soy sauce, tomato ketchup, sherry, five-spice
powder and sugar. Cover
and marinate for 1 1/2
hours in the refrigerator.
2 Heat the oil, add the
pork and stir-fry until
evenly browned. Mix in
the vegetables and stir-fry
for 3 minutes.
3 Add the stock, season
with salt, pepper and chilli
oil, then bring to the boil.
Lower the heat, cover and
simmer for 45 minutes.
4 Stir in the cornflour,
bring to the boil and simmer for 1 minute.

*Photograph opposite
(bottom right)*

Pork Strips with White Cabbage

Serves 4
Preparation time: 1 hour
2120 kcal/8905 kJ

---

30 ml/2 tbsp groundnut oil

450 g/1 lb pork, cut into
strips

2 onions, sliced

2 red peppers, cut into
strips

450 g/1 lb white cabbage,
shredded

6 Chinese mushrooms,
soaked and cut into strips

2 cloves garlic, chopped

2 pieces stem ginger in
syrup, chopped

30 ml/2 tbsp honey

45 ml/3 tbsp soy sauce

120 ml/4 fl oz/1/4 cup dry
white wine

salt and pepper

10 ml/2 tsp cornflour mixed
with 15 ml/1 tbsp water

---

1 Heat the oil in a wok and
quickly brown the pork,
stirring continuously.
3 Add the vegetables,
garlic and ginger and
quickly fry together.
3 Add the honey, soy
sauce and wine. Bring to
the boil, cover and simmer
over a moderate heat for
40 minutes until the meat
is cooked.
4 Season to taste with salt
and pepper, and stir in the
cornflour mixture. Bring
just up to the boil, stirring
continuously, and simmer
for 1 minute.

*Photograph opposite
(bottom left)*

Pork in Red Sauce

Serves 4
Preparation time: 40 mins
2420 kcal/10165 kJ

---

30 ml/2 tbsp groundnut oil

225 g/8 oz prepared pork
kidneys, cut into strips

450 g/1 lb pork, cut into
strips

1 onion, sliced

1 bunch spring onions, cut
into strips

2 carrots, cut into strips

1 stalk celery, cut into strips

1 red pepper, cut into
narrow strips

45 ml/3 tbsp soy sauce

50 ml/2 fl oz/1/4 cup dry
white wine

300 ml/1/2 pt/1 1/4 cups
chicken or beef stock

30 ml/2 tbsp plum sauce

30 ml/2 tbsp vinegar

5 ml/1 tsp five-spice powder

5 ml/1 tsp brown sugar

15 ml/1 tbsp cornflour mixed
with 15 ml/1 tbsp water

---

1 Heat the oil and fry the
kidneys, stirring. Remove
the kidneys from the wok.
2 Fry the pork in the re-
maining fat, stirring.
3 Add the vegetables
and fry. Add the soy
sauce, wine, stock, plum
sauce, vinegar, five-spice
powder and sugar. Bring
to the boil, cover and simmer for 30 minutes unt
cooked. Add the kidney
and season.
4 Add the cornflour and
bring to the boil, stirring
continuously. Simmer fo
1 minute.
Photograph opposite (top

Steamed Far Eastern Dishes

A gentle form of cooking, steaming is a traditional Chinese method of preparing meat, vegetables and either sweet or savoury dumplings. The food is generally steamed in a bamboo basket, placed inside or on top of the wok.

Filled Yeast Dumplings,
page 58

Yeast Dumplings

Serves 4
Preparation time: 1 1/2 hours plus cooling
2540 kcal/10670 kJ

Dough:

450 g/1 lb plain white flour

1 sachet easy-mix yeast

10 ml/2 tsp caster sugar

5 ml/1 tsp salt

300 ml/1/2 pt/1 1/4 cups warm milk or water

Filling:

30 ml/2 tbsp groundnut oil

225 g/8 oz ground beef

1 onion, chopped

2 pieces stem ginger in syrup, chopped

50 g/2 oz cashews, chopped

2.5 ml/1/2 tsp five-spice powder

15 ml/1 tbsp soy sauce

30 ml/2 tbsp Hoisin sauce

2.5 ml/1/2 tsp vinegar

salt and Szechuan pepper

15 ml/1 tbsp cornflour

45 ml/3 tbsp cold water

1 Mix the dough ingredients into an elastic mixture. Cover and leave to rise in a warm place for about 45 minutes.
3 Heat the oil and fry the meat until golden brown.
3 Add next seven ingredients and bring to the boil. Season, and simmer for 2 minutes. Cool.
4 Shape the dough into 16 balls. Press flat, spoon some filling in each, and close into balls. Put into the steam basket in the wok, cover and steam over salted water for 20 to 30 minutes.
Photograph page 56

Marinated Steamed Vegetables

Serves 4
Preparation time: 30 mins plus marinating
780 kcal/3275 kJ

225 g/8 oz broccoli florets

225 g/8 oz cauliflower florets

100 g/4 oz fresh oyster mushrooms

2 carrots, thinly sliced

1 stalk celery, thinly sliced

30 ml/2 tbsp groundnut oil

Marinade:

1 wine glass dry white wine

30 ml/2 tbsp plum sauce

30 ml/2 tbsp soy sauce

juice of 1 orange

5 ml/1 tsp Szechuan pepper, coarsely ground

30 ml/2 tbsp vinegar

1 Heat the oil in a wok, add the vegetables and stir-fry for 5 to 6 minutes.
2 Remove the vegetables from the wok, and put them in a bowl. Combine the marinade ingredients, add to the vegetables, toss well to mix. Cover and refrigerate overnight.
3 Place the marinated vegetables into the steamer, cover and cook in the wok for about 15 minutes over gently boiling water to which 30-45 ml/2 to 3 tbsp vinegar have been added.

Photograph opposite (top)

Steamed Minced Meatballs

Serves 4
Preparation time: 35 mins
2535 kcal/10650 kJ

2 cloves garlic

salt

500 g/1 1/4 lb minced lean pork (loin is an excellent choice)

1 onion, finely chopped

1 red pepper, chopped

1 green pepper, chopped

2 pieces stem ginger in syrup, chopped

5 ml/1 tsp curry powder

5 ml/1 tsp paprika

1 egg, beaten

30-45 ml/2-3 tbsp cornflour

50 g/2 oz round grain rice, raw

Szechuan pepper

60 ml/4 tbsp chopped chives

1 Crush the garlic with the salt and combine thoroughly with the pork onion, peppers, ginger curry and paprika.
2 Work the egg into the mixture with the cornflour and rice. Season to taste with salt and pepper, then mix in the chives.
3 With wet hands, shape the mixture into small balls. Place these in the steam basket, cover and cook in the wok over gently boiling water for 20 to 25 minutes.

Photograph opposite (bottom)

Steamed Fish Plait

Serves 4
Preparation time: 1 hour
1240 kcal/5210 kJ

---

500 g/1 ¹/₄ lb haddock fillets, skinned

---

salt

---

*5 ml/1 **tsp** five-spice powder*

---

juice of 2 lemons

Marinade:
*5 ml/1 **tsp** aniseed, coarsely ground*

---

*5 ml/1 **tsp** Szechuan pepper, coarsely ground*

---

*30 ml/**2 tbsp** soy sauce*

---

*30 ml/**2 tbsp** oyster sauce*

---

*15 ml/1 **tbsp** honey*

---

*60 ml/**4 tbsp** chives, chopped*

8-10 large sorrel or spinach leaves

---

*30-45 ml/**2-3 tbsp** vinegar*

---

1 Cut the fish fillets into long, thin strips and form into plaits. Sprinkle with salt, five-spice powder and lemon juice. Transfer to a bowl.
2 Combine all the marinade ingredients. Pour over the fish plaits and leave to marinate for at least 30 minutes.
3 Line the steam basket with the sorrel or spinach leaves. Place the plaits in the basket, cover and cook in the wok for 20 to 25 minutes over gently boiling water to which vinegar has been added.

Photograph (bottom)

Steamed Fish Roulades

Serves 4
Preparation time: 1 hour
1770 kcal/7435 kJ

500 g/1 ¼ **lb** haddock fillets, skinned and diced

Marinade:
juice of 1 lemon

30 ml/**2 tbsp** soy sauce

30 ml/**2 tbsp** oyster sauce

30 ml/**2 tbsp** plum sauce

dash of Chinese rice wine or dry sherry

salt and Szechuan pepper

100 g/**4 oz** beansprouts

100 g/**4 oz** green peas

6 Chinese mushrooms, soaked and cut into strips

50 g/**2 oz** walnuts, chopped

1 egg, beaten

30 ml/**2 tbsp** cornflour

1 small head of Chinese cabbage, blanched

vinegar water

1 Put the diced fish into a bowl. Combine the marinade ingredients, pour over the fish and marinate for 30 minutes.
2 Add the vegetables, nuts, beaten egg and cornflour. Mix and season.
3 Lay 3 Chinese leaves on top of each other, spoon on some fish mixture and roll up. Continue until all ingredients are used up.
4 Place rolls in steam basket, cover and cook in wok for 30 minutes over simmering water with 30-45 ml/2-3 tbsp vinegar.

Photograph (top)

Steamed Meat Pudding

Serves 4
Preparation time: 30 mins
2410 kcal/10120 kJ

---

500 g/1 ¼ lb mixture of minced pork and beef

1 onion, diced

6 Chinese mushrooms, soaked and diced

30 ml/2 tbsp mango chutney

30 ml/2 tbsp Hoisin sauce

30 ml/2 tbsp soy sauce

5 ml/1 tsp five-spice powder

1 clove of garlic, crushed

5 ml/1 tsp salt

1 egg, beaten

30-45 ml/2-3 tbsp cornflour

Szechuan pepper

60 ml/4 tbsp chopped chives

8-10 large dark green cabbage leaves

300 ml/½ pt/1 ¼ cups meat stock

---

1 Put the mince, onion, mushrooms, chutney, sauces, spice and garlic into a bowl and work to a soft mixture. Season.
2 Add the egg and cornflour, season with pepper and mix in the chives.
3 Line the steam basket with the cabbage leaves. Form the mince into a cake shape, and place on the leaves. Cover.
4 Cook the meat pudding in the wok over a well-seasoned meat stock for 25 to 30 minutes.

Photograph opposite (top)

Sweet Ginger Balls

Serves 4
Preparation time: 1½ hours
2630 kcal/11045 kJ

Dough:
450 g/1 lb strong plain white flour

25 g/1 oz/2 tbsp margarine

15 ml/1 tbsp caster sugar

2.5 ml/½ tsp salt

1 sachet easy-mix dried yeast

300 ml/½ pt/1 ¼ cups warm milk or water

Filling:
25 g/1 oz walnuts, chopped

50 g/2 oz chopped mixed peel

50 g/2 oz glacé cherries, chopped

50 g/2 oz stoned dates, chopped

15 ml/1 tbsp Chinese rice wine or medium sherry

a pinch of powdered ginger

---

slightly sugared water

---

1 Sift the flour into a bowl. Rub in the margarine then add the remaining dough ingredients. Knead well to workable and elastic mixture then cover and leave to rise in a warm place for about 45 minutes.
2 Mix all the filling ingredients well together.

3 Quickly re-knead the dough. Shape it into 16 to 18 small balls. Press them flat, spoon some of the filling into each and close the balls firmly by pinching the edges well together.
4 Place the balls in a bamboo steam basket, cover and leave to rise again in a warm place.
5 Heat slightly sweetened water in a wok. Place the steam basket over the water, cover and steam the balls for 20 to 30 minutes.

Photograph opposite (bottom)

Variation
Those who enjoy the taste of ginger can also fill the balls with the following mixture: 50 g/2 oz finely chopped ginger stems in syrup, 50 g/2 oz flaked almonds and 50 g/2 oz raisins, a little powdered ginger and 30 ml/1 tbsp ginger wine.

Index of Recipes

Foulsham
Yeovil Road, Slough, Berkshire, SL1 4JH
ISBN 0-572-01661-1
This English language edition copyright
© 1991 W. Foulsham & Co. Ltd.
Originally published by Falken-Verlag,
GmbH, Niedernhausen TS, West
Germany.
Photographs copyright © Falken Verlag

Printed in Portugal